COTTON

THE COOKBOOK

COTTON

THE COOKBOOK

Jeffrey Paige

PHOTOGRAPHS BY BRIAN SMESTAD :: FOREWORD BY JOHN CLAYTON

Blue Tree
PORTSMOUTH

First published in the United States in 2009
by Blue Tree, LLC
P.O. Box 148
Portsmouth, NH 03802

37 10 1

Printed in Hong Kong

Library of Congress
Cataloging-in-Publication Data
2008937899

Cotton: The Cookbook
Jeffrey Paige
Photographs by Brian Smestad
Foreword by John Clayton

ISBN-10: 0-9802245-2-7
ISBN-13: 978-0-9802245-2-8

For customer service, orders, and book projects:
Local 603.436.0831
Toll-Free 866.852.5357
Email sales@TheBlueTree.com

www.TheBlueTree.com

Blue Tree
AN ARTISTIC PUBLISHING COMPANY

═ Contents ═

= Foreword =

I'll never forget my first meal in Manchester, New Hampshire's Millyard. In the early 1960s, my father was a plumber at the Waumbec Mill, a textile operation that rose from the ashes of what was once the world's largest textile concern, Manchester's famed Amoskeag Manufacturing Corporation.

As a kid, I was fascinated by the red brick buildings that lined the Merrimack River, and on Saturdays—ordinarily a day for my dad to pick up some overtime—I would tag along with him. That's how I first came to eat at the Millyard.

The mills were steam-powered in those days, so when the lunch hour came, my dad would head down to the boiler room. While other employees had to resort to the old-fashioned thermos bottle if they wanted hot soup, my father simply opened a can, poured the contents into a pan he kept in his locker, and then set the pan on a white-hot steam pipe. Minutes later, we were eating a hot lunch, and I thought that bowl of Habitant pea soup—canned just two mill buildings to the north—was as close as I'd ever get to heaven.

Of course, my father wasn't the first epicurean adventurer on Manchester's labor scene. Back when W.H. McElwain was the largest shoe manufacturer in the world, a Simmons College graduate named Helen Siebold was serving more than 2,000 meals a day at the McElwain plant.

They christened her the "Shoe-Shop Chef." In reporting on her exploits, the *Boston Herald Traveler* noted that, "By careful planning, Miss Siebold is able to offer her factory people a three-course meal for the ridiculous sum of twenty-five cents. There is always a soup, a meat and a vegetable dish, or a nourishing meat substitute, and a choice of desserts, which include pudding and four kinds of ice cream." "Now, shoe workers who scoffed at the idea of a college girl knowing how to make a good beef stew and pie," the paper added, "have found this matter-of-fact person to be the best chef they ever knew." Ah, but those shoe workers didn't know Jeffrey Paige.

Dining in Manchester's Millyard has come a long way since the days of Helen Siebold—let alone my father—and Jeff is one of the reasons. In the early fall of 2000, Jeff opened Cotton, a dining establishment of both style and substance, in a building that speaks volumes about Manchester's industrial heritage.

The restaurant is housed in a former blacksmith shop that was one of the many outbuildings of the Amoskeag Corporation's world-renowned machine shop. Every bit of industrial hardware that was required for the creation

of textiles was forged there, beginning with looms, spoolers, and warpers. Later on, the machine shop churned out giant turbine water wheels, then railroad locomotives and steam fire engines. During the Civil War, when the supply of raw cotton was curtailed by the rebelling Confederate States, Amoskeag agent Ezekiel Straw called upon his good friend, President Abraham Lincoln. To aid the Union cause, Straw volunteered to retool the Amoskeag machine shop to manufacture Springfield rifles—workers who made those rifles were exempt from the Union draft, incidentally—and the metal for those rifles was forged in the blacksmith shop that is now home to Cotton. The place is alive with history, yes, but thanks to Jeff Paige and his wife and partner, Christine "Peaches" Paige, that vibrant past is equaled by a future of great promise.

In the eight years since they first opened their doors, they have repeatedly been honored with *New Hampshire Magazine's* "Best of New Hampshire" awards. But Cotton is not just some local phenomenon. *Yankee* magazine called it "one of New England's not-to-miss restaurants," then *Bon Appétit* told its readers that Cotton was, "one of the top-ten neighborhood restaurants in the Northeast," and, when the August *New York Times* proclaimed it to be "a hip bistro," there was no denying Cotton's place in the pantheon of American dining. Behind it all is Jeff.

The New Hampshire native is a graduate of the prestigious Culinary Institute of America in Hyde Park, New York, but it is his appreciation for New England's rich culinary history that was the inspiration for creating the award-winning dining experience at Canterbury Shaker Village. That twelve-year labor of love resulted in two best-selling cookbooks. The first was *Cooking in the Shaker Spirit*, which Jeff co-authored with renowned chef James Haller. Then came a solo effort, *The Shaker Kitchen: Over 100 Recipes from Canterbury Shaker Village*, which was published by Random House in April of 1994 and has sold more than 100,000 copies.

And now comes this. "We like to think we understand Manchester and the Millyard," Jeff said. "There's such a great tradition here—a tangible work ethic—and with Cotton, we worked to create a restaurant that expresses that understanding. When you use higher quality ingredients, people instinctively think 'fine dining,' and there's nothing wrong with fine dining, but we like to tell people we offer comfort food." And then some.

—John Clayton

= Introduction =

I don't know how or why, but I always knew I wanted to be a cook—a chef is, first and foremost, a cook. My journey had humble beginnings, like most chefs in this profession. I started washing dishes at age thirteen. Not a glamorous job, by any means, but it offered a glimpse into what my future held for me. It was hard work, with long days and nights, cramped and steamy quarters, a fast-paced environment often riddled with stressful moments—it was controlled chaos, to be honest, but I loved every minute of it and still do.

I've since graduated to restaurateur. More often than not, though, you'll find me in the kitchen cooking at one of the stations. Cooking is my true love, owning a restaurant a distant second.

Cotton opened in the fall of 2000. Located in Manchester's Historic Millyard District, Cotton is known for exceptional food, friendly yet professional service, and an inviting, casual, upscale atmosphere. The cooking is sophisticated and eclectic, seasonal comfort food. Robust plates are created with distinct flavors and presented in a straightforward manner, allowing the quality of the ingredients to speak for themselves. Cotton has an extensive and always changing wine list, over forty wines by the glass, and holds the distinct honor of offering the "best martinis in New Hampshire" five years in a row according to *New Hampshire Magazine*.

The book you hold before you is but a snapshot of a restaurant called Cotton. As a small token of our appreciation for you, our cherished guests, we present twenty-five of our most requested recipes. We truly appreciate all of you who join us at Cotton. We wouldn't be here without you.

—Jeffrey Paige

= Appetizers =

Appetizers, hors d'oeuvres, small plates, tapas, meze, antipasti, etc., are the international names for simple "snacks" or "tastes" that tantalize the taste buds before a meal. Today, more and more people are creating entire dinners out of these little "tastes." The recipes included here can all be easily adapted to any dining needs: served as individual appetizers, offered buffet-style, or passed on trays for a party or event.

Pan-Fried Crab Cakes

with Chipotle-Honey Aioli and Black Bean Corn Salsa

1 pound Maine crabmeat, picked over for shells
1 pound lump crabmeat, picked over for shells
1½ cups fresh breadcrumbs
½ cup mayonnaise
1½ tablespoons Dijon-style mustard
1½ tablespoons fresh lemon juice
1 teaspoon kosher salt
1 teaspoon coarse-ground black pepper
1 teaspoon onion powder
3 scallions, thinly sliced, green stalks only
1 extra-large egg
¼ cup vegetable oil
1 cup dried breadcrumbs

CHIPOTLE-HONEY AIOLI
3 to 4 chipotle peppers in adobo sauce
1 tablespoon honey
1 cup mayonnaise

BLACK BEAN CORN SALSA
Two 15-ounce cans black beans, drained and rinsed
2 cups fresh or frozen corn kernels
½ cup small diced green bell pepper
½ cup small diced red bell pepper
¼ cup small diced red onion
1 tablespoon chopped garlic
1 level teaspoon ground cumin
1 level teaspoon ground light chili powder
½ teaspoon Tabasco sauce
¼ cup vegetable oil
2 tablespoons cider vinegar
1 tablespoon chopped fresh cilantro
Kosher salt and fresh-ground black pepper, to taste

Gently drain the excess water from the crabmeat. In a mixing bowl, whisk together the mayonnaise, mustard, lemon juice, salt, pepper, onion powder, scallions, and egg.

In a large mixing bowl, gently combine the crabmeat, fresh breadcrumbs, and wet ingredients, being careful not to overmix. Shape the mixture into twelve cakes, about ⅓ cup each. Transfer the cakes to a wax paper-lined baking sheet. Cover and chill at least 4 hours, but no more than 1 day.

Preheat oven to 250°F. Gently coat each crab cake in the dried breadcrumbs. Heat the oil in a large sauté pan over medium-high heat. Add half of the crab cakes and cook until golden-brown, approximately 3 to 4 minutes per side. Transfer to a sheet pan and hold in the oven while you cook the remaining crab cakes.

To serve, place ½ cup of salsa on each plate, two crab cakes on top of the salsa, and top with a dollop of the aioli. Serve immediately.

CHIPOTLE-HONEY AIOLI
Combine the chipotle peppers and honey in a blender and mix until smooth. Press the mixture through a strainer to remove the seeds. In a mixing bowl, combine the chipotle-honey purée with the mayonnaise. Refrigerate until ready to serve.

BLACK BEAN CORN SALSA
In a large mixing bowl, combine the black beans, corn, bell peppers, and red onion. In a small mixing bowl, combine the remaining ingredients and mix well. Gently fold the liquid mixture into the beans and vegetables, incorporating. Adjust the seasoning with kosher salt and pepper. Refrigerate until ready to serve.

Bruschetta

with Fresh Mozzarella, Balsamic Marinated Tomatoes, and Basil Aioli

½ loaf Italian bread
Extra-virgin olive oil
1 large garlic clove, peeled
One 8-ounce ball fresh mozzarella
1 recipe Balsamic Marinated Tomatoes (*recipe follows*)
1 recipe Basil Aioli (*recipe follows*)

BALSAMIC MARINATED TOMATOES

8 fresh plum tomatoes
1 tablespoon chopped garlic
2 tablespoons extra-virgin olive oil
¾ cup balsamic vinegar
12 to 15 fresh basil leaves, cut into thin strips
Kosher salt and fresh-ground pepper, to taste

BASIL AIOLI

Makes about 1 cup
1 cup mayonnaise
½ cup fresh basil leaves, lightly packed

Preheat gas grill or oven to 400°F. Cut the bread into 6 to 8 slices, ¾-inch thick. Brush both sides of the bread with olive oil and grill until golden-brown on both sides, or toast in the oven. Carefully rub each slice of toasted bread with the fresh garlic clove. Cut mozzarella into even pieces equal to the number of bread slices. Top each piece of bread with a slice of fresh mozzarella, spoon the tomato mixture over the mozzarella, dividing evenly, and finish each with a dollop of basil aioli. Serve immediately.

BALSAMIC MARINATED TOMATOES

Wash, core, seed, and chop the tomatoes into ½-inch dice. In a mixing bowl, combine the diced tomatoes, garlic, olive oil, balsamic vinegar, and basil, tossing well. Season to taste with kosher salt and fresh-ground black pepper. Cover and refrigerate for 4 to 6 hours. Return to room temperature before serving.

BASIL AIOLI

Heat a small pot of lightly salted water to a boil. Add the basil leaves and cook for 10 seconds. Strain and immediately shock them in a bowl of ice water. Gently squeeze most of the water out of the leaves. Place the blanched basil into a blender and process until it produces a smooth purée. In a mixing bowl, stir the basil purée into the mayonnaise. Season with kosher salt. Refrigerate.

Heirloom Tomato Stack

with Fresh Mozzarella, Pistachio Pesto, and Balsamic Syrup   SERVES 4

4 heirloom tomatoes
Two 8-ounce fresh mozzarella balls
1 recipe Pistachio Pesto
1 recipe Balsamic Syrup

PISTACHIO PESTO
Makes about 1¼ cups
¼ cup shelled pistachio nuts
1 teaspoon chopped garlic
2 cups lightly packed Genovese basil leaves
½ cup vegetable oil
¼ cup olive oil
½ cup grated pecorino or Parmesan cheese
Kosher salt and fresh-ground pepper to taste

BALSAMIC SYRUP
1 cup balsamic vinegar
2 level tablespoons sugar

We only run this salad for a few weeks each year, late August to early September, when New Hampshire tomatoes are at their peak. Nesenkeag Farm grows several types of heirloom tomatoes and the variety changes from year to year at the farm manager's whim. This year he's growing Brandywine, Cherokee Purple, German Johnson, Nebraska Wedding, Persimmon, Red Calabash, and Dr. Wyche's, to name just a few.

For this salad, feel free to mix and match varieties. The taste and color contrasts will surely wow your dinner guests.

Core and slice each tomato into 4 even slices, keeping each tomato together on your cutting board. Slice each mozzarella ball into 6 even slices. Stack each tomato on a serving plate, starting with a slice of tomato, slice of mozzarella, drizzle of pesto, slice of tomato, slice of mozzarella, etc., ending with a tomato slice—each stack should have 4 tomato slices and 3 slices of mozzarella. Drizzle additional pesto and a little of the Balsamic Syrup around the plate and serve.

PISTACHIO PESTO
In the bowl of a food processor, combine the pistachio nuts, garlic, and basil leaves. Process until the mixture is finely chopped. Add the oils and cheese, pulsing just until the cheese is incorporated. Season to taste with kosher salt and fresh-ground black pepper. Refrigerate, will keep up to 3 days.

BALSAMIC SYRUP
In a heavy-bottom saucepan, combine the vinegar and sugar. Heat to a boil and reduce the heat to a low simmer. Cook, approximately 20 to 30 minutes, until reduced by ⅔ or a syrup-like consistency. Remove from the heat and cool completely. Store covered, up to 1 month.

Grilled Marinated Vegetable Antipasto

Serves 6 to 8

1 medium zucchini
1 medium summer squash
1 tablespoon chopped garlic
¼ cup vegetable oil
1 cup balsamic vinegar
Two 8-ounce balls fresh mozzarella, each cut into 6 slices
1 recipe Balsamic Marinated Tomatoes (*see page 17*)
1 recipe Basil Aioli (*see page 17*)

Slice the zucchini and summer squash into ¼-inch thick rounds. In a large mixing bowl, combine the zucchini and summer squash with the garlic, vegetable oil, and balsamic vinegar, tossing well. Cover and refrigerate 4 to 6 hours.

Preheat your outdoor grill. Grill the squashes, approximately 2 to 3 minutes per side, being careful not to overcook. The squash should still have a little "bite" to them. Transfer to a platter and refrigerate until ready to serve.

This dish can either be served on individual plates or presented family-style on a large serving platter. Start with a ring of overlapping zucchini slices, followed by a ring of summer squash. Continue until all of the zucchini and summer squash are used. Place a ring of overlapping mozzarella slices on top of the zucchini and summer squash. Place the Balsamic Marinated Tomatoes in the center of the plate. Sprinkle the entire dish with a little kosher salt and black pepper. Drizzle the aioli over all or serve on the side.

Pan-Seared Scallops

with Mesclun Greens, Balsamic Vinaigrette, Crushed Pistachios, Tomatoes, and Crumbled Bleu Cheese Serves 4 to 6

One 7-ounce package organic spring salad mix
½ recipe Balsamic Vinaigrette (*see page 39*)
½ cup shelled pistachio nuts, crushed
8 grape or cherry tomatoes, cut into quarters lengthwise
One 4-ounce container crumbled bleu cheese
2 pounds U 20-30 count fresh dry pack sea scallops
1 tablespoon vegetable oil
Kosher salt and fresh-ground black pepper, to taste

Our sea scallops are harvested off the Northeast coastline from Newfoundland to New Bedford, Massachusetts, and are referred to in the industry as "day boat" or "dry pack" scallops. Scallops cannot survive long out of the water so they are usually shucked on the boat shortly after harvest and kept on ice until delivered to shoreside, all-natural and chemical free. "Wet pack" scallops, which are never served at Cotton, have routinely been treated with a water phosphate solution to prevent the scallops from losing water and shrinking. This process actually causes the scallops to soak up additional water—increasing their weight by up to twenty-five percent—and since water is cheaper than scallops, there is a powerful economic incentive to sell/serve "soaked or wet pack" scallops. Also they tend to boil or steam when pan-seared rather than caramelizing to form that nice golden crust. Get to know your fish monger and your scallops.

Scallops are sorted and sold by their size. U-10 scallops means approximately 10 scallops to the pound. U 20-30 means approximately 20 to 30 scallops to the pound.

Heat the vegetable oil in a large sauté pan over high heat. Season the scallops with kosher salt and black pepper. Carefully add the scallops, being careful not to crowd the pan, cooking until the bottoms begin to caramelize, 3 to 4 minutes. Flip the scallops and cook an additional 2 to 3 minutes.

While the scallops are cooking, combine the spring salad mix, pistachio nuts, tomatoes, and crumbled bleu cheese in a large mixing bowl. Add the dressing and gently toss. Evenly divide the salad mixture among the serving plates. Place the hot scallops around the salad and serve immediately.

═ Soups ═

The soul-satisfying recipes included here take you through the entire cooking year. What says summer in New England better than a bowl of chowder made with native corn and lobster? You can also beat the heat with a refreshing bowl of chilled Watermelon Gazpacho.

As the days grow shorter, you can take the chill out of the New England autumn air with our Harvest Cider Pumpkin Soup—and it certainly wouldn't be winter at Cotton without an oven-baked crock of Onion Apple Cider Soup to warm you to the bone.

Baked Onion Apple Cider Soup

with Smoked Cheddar Cheese Gratiné

1 stick unsalted butter
5 medium onions, peeled and thinly sliced
4 cups beef stock
4 cups fresh apple cider
2 teaspoons minced fresh thyme
¼ cup light brown sugar (*omit if cider is sweet enough*)
Kosher salt and fresh-ground black pepper, to taste
Butter as needed for spreading
6 to 8 slices of French bread, ¼-inch thick
6 to 8 slices of Gruyère or Swiss cheese
2 cups grated smoked Vermont cheddar
   or traditional cheddar cheese

In a large saucepan, melt the butter over medium-low heat. Add the onions and cook until well caramelized, about 20 to 30 minutes, taking care not to burn them. Add the stock, cider, and thyme, bring the soup to a boil, then lower the heat and simmer the soup for 1½ hours. Skim the top of the soup periodically. Season the soup with the brown sugar, if needed, and salt and pepper. The soup may be made up to this point a day ahead and kept covered in the refrigerator.

To make the croutons, lightly butter the slices of French bread and broil until toasted on both sides. To serve, preheat the oven to 400°F. Place 6 to 8 ovenproof soup cups or crocks in a large roasting pan and fill them with the hot soup. Pour hot water into the roasting pan to come halfway up the sides of the cups or crocks. Top each cup or crock of soup with a crouton, a slice of Gruyere cheese, and ⅓ to ¼ cup of grated cheddar. Bake the soup until the cheese is golden-brown and the soup is hot and bubbly. Serve immediately.

Sherried Maine Lobster Bisque

Two 1¼-pound cooked lobsters (*ask your fish monger to cook them for you*)

1 stick unsalted butter

10 tablespoons all-purpose flour

6 cups lobster stock (*recipe follows*)

2 cups cream sherry

1 cup heavy cream

2 tablespoons chopped parsley

Kosher salt and ground white pepper, to taste

LOBSTER STOCK

Makes about 1½ quarts

1 tablespoon vegetable oil

Two 1¼-pound lobster bodies

1 small onion, peeled and chopped

1 small carrot, chopped

2 celery ribs, chopped

2 tablespoons tomato paste

2 bay leaves

6 to 8 whole peppercorns

2 quarts cold water

Kosher salt, to taste

Crack the lobster tails, knuckles, claws, and legs, and remove the meat. Coarsely chop the meat and refrigerate. Save the lobster bodies for the lobster stock.

In a large soup pot, melt the butter over medium heat, add the flour, and stir to combine. Cook for 2 to 3 minutes, stirring constantly. Stir in the stock, whisking constantly to avoid lumps. Heat to a boil, reduce to a low simmer, and cook for 30 minutes, stirring often.

In a separate saucepan, cook the cream sherry until reduced by half. Be careful during the cooking process, as the sherry may ignite. The flame will extinguish itself when the alcohol content has cooked off. Stir into the large soup pot the reduced cream sherry, heavy cream, and chopped parsley, and season to taste with kosher salt and ground white pepper.

To serve, evenly divide the chopped lobster meat among the serving bowls. Ladle the hot soup over the lobster meat and serve immediately.

LOBSTER STOCK

Remove the head sacs and tomalleys from the lobster bodies and discard. In a large saucepot, heat the oil over medium-high heat. Add the bodies and cook for 5 minutes, stirring often. Add the remaining ingredients, except the water, and cook for an additional 5 minutes, stirring often. Add the cold water and bring to a boil, then simmer for 1 hour, skimming the foam that floats to the top. Season the stock with kosher salt. Strain. Cool stock completely and store covered in the refrigerator, will keep up to 3 days.

Maine Lobster Corn Chowder

½ pound smoked bacon, diced
1 medium onion, peeled and diced small
1½ pounds red potatoes, washed
2 bay leaves
4 to 5 cups chicken, lobster, or vegetable stock
2 cups fresh corn
2 cups chopped cooked lobster meat
2 tablespoons chopped parsley
1 cup heavy cream
Kosher salt and fresh-ground black pepper, to taste

Nothing says summer in New England like fresh corn on the cob and boiled lobster. Here we've combined the two summertime staples to make a delicious chowder.

In a large saucepan, fry the bacon over medium heat just until it starts to crisp, about 8 to 10 minutes. Meanwhile, quarter and slice the potatoes ¼ inch thick. Set aside. Add the onion and bay leaves to the bacon and cook until the onion is translucent, about 3 to 5 minutes. Carefully drain off half of the bacon grease and discard. Add the potatoes to a saucepot and enough stock to cover them, and bring to a simmer over medium heat. Simmer until the potatoes are tender, about 10 minutes. Add the corn, lobster meat, parsley, and heavy cream, and cook until heated through, stirring often. Remove the bay leaves. Season with kosher salt and black pepper, and serve.

Watermelon Gazpacho

SERVES 4 TO 6

5 pounds red seedless watermelon
½ cup finely diced red onion
1 cup finely diced red bell pepper
2 cups diced, peeled, and seeded cucumber
½ jalapeño pepper, seeds removed and finely chopped
1 tablespoon chopped fresh cilantro
1 tablespoon chopped fresh parsley
¼ cup red wine vinegar
¼ cup granular sugar
Kosher salt, to taste

Remove the rind from the watermelon and cut into 1-inch chunks. Purée in a food processor until fairly smooth. Transfer to a large mixing bowl. Add the remaining ingredients and stir to blend well. Season to taste with kosher salt. Refrigerate 4 hours before serving. Serve within 2 days of making.

Harvest Cider Pumpkin Soup

SERVES 4 TO 6

1 stick unsalted butter
10 tablespoons all-purpose flour
1 quart apple cider
1 quart chicken or vegetable stock
One 15-ounce can pumpkin purée
¼ cup light brown sugar
1 teaspoon ground cinnamon
1½ cups heavy cream
Kosher salt and ground white pepper, to taste

In a large saucepan, melt the butter over medium heat. Add the flour and stir to combine. Cook for 2 to 3 minutes, stirring constantly. Stir in the cider and stock, whisking constantly to avoid lumps. Add the brown sugar, pumpkin purée, and cinnamon, stirring to incorporate. Heat to a boil, reduce to a low simmer, and cook for 30 minutes, stirring often. Add the heavy cream and season to taste with kosher salt and ground white pepper, and serve.

$=$ Salads $=$

Summertime is salad time, when native produce is at its peak of quantity, quality, and variety. Most of my salads start with a base of Nesenkeag Farm's organic greens: baby spinach, baby arugula, or their mesclun, an ever-changing, seasonally driven mixture of baby lettuces, greens, herbs, and edible flowers. The greens are tossed with a housemade dressing or vinaigrette. I like to incorporate fresh or dried fruit or seasonal vegetables for color and contrast of texture and taste. The salad is finished with toasted, seasoned nuts and often a bit of cheese.

Turn any of these salads into an entrée salad with the simple addition of grilled chicken, shrimp, or fish, such as salmon, tuna, or swordfish.

An old friend once said to me, "No cook is really good without a lively imagination and the will to use it." The possibilities are endless with summertime salads.

Nesenkeag Farm's Organic Mesclun Salad

with Balsamic Vinaigrette

BALSAMIC VINAIGRETTE
Makes 1¾ cups
1 cup soybean salad oil
1 tablespoon Dijon mustard
½ cup balsamic vinegar
¼ cup granular sugar
¼ teaspoon kosher salt
Pinch fresh-ground black pepper

Nesenkeag Farm, located in Litchfield, New Hampshire, is one of our state's oldest and largest certified organic vegetable farms. From late May through early November, we purchase a variety of pristine produce from them, including herbs, mesclun salad mix, braising greens, baby arugula, baby spinach, tri-colored beets, heirloom tomatoes, and potatoes, to name a few.

Our house salad is their wonderful, ever-changing mesclun mixture: organic baby lettuce, spinach, greens, herbs, and edible flowers.

Serve this dressing with a mixture of simple salad greens from your own garden or area farmer's market.

Combine all of the ingredients in a food processor or blender. Pulse just until the ingredients become emulsified. Refrigerate. Will keep for up to 5 days refrigerated.

Organic Baby Arugula Salad

with Strawberries, Red Onions, Feta, Toasted Almonds, and White Balsamic Vinaigrette SERVES 6 TO 8

⅓ cup vegetable oil

⅓ cup white balsamic vinegar

Three 5-ounce packages organic baby arugula

1 pint fresh strawberries, stems removed, quartered

1 small red onion, peeled, cut in half, and thinly sliced

One 6-ounce container crumbled feta cheese
   (*may substitute with goat cheese*)

½ cup toasted slivered almonds

Kosher salt and fresh-ground black pepper, to taste

In a small mixing bowl, combine the vegetable oil and white balsamic vinegar. Whisk to combine well. Season to taste with kosher salt and fresh-ground black pepper. In a large mixing bowl, combine the arugula, strawberries, and red onions. Gently toss with the vinaigrette. Divide the arugula mixture evenly among the serving plates, and top each with the crumbled feta and toasted slivered almonds. Serve immediately.

Organic Baby Spinach Salad

with Blueberries, Red Onions, Bleu Cheese, Toasted Almonds, and Maple Balsamic Vinaigrette   SERVES 6 TO 8

1 recipe Maple Balsamic Vinaigrette (*recipe follows*)
Two 11-ounce packages organic baby spinach
1 pint fresh blueberries, washed, stems removed
1 small red onion, peeled, cut in half, and thinly sliced
One 6-ounce container crumbled bleu cheese
½ cup toasted slivered almonds
Kosher salt and fresh-ground black pepper, to taste

MAPLE BALSAMIC VINAIGRETTE
Makes 1¼ cups
½ cup maple syrup
½ cup vegetable oil
½ cup balsamic vinegar
1 teaspoon Dijon-style mustard
Kosher salt and fresh-ground black pepper, to taste

In a large mixing bowl, combine the spinach, red onion, and blueberries. Gently toss with the vinaigrette. Divide the spinach mixture amongst the serving plates and top each with the crumbled bleu cheese and toasted slivered almonds. Serve immediately.

MAPLE BALSAMIC VINAIGRETTE
Combine all of the ingredients in a blender and process until well incorporated. Season to taste and refrigerate.

The Wedge

1 large head of iceberg lettuce, quartered
1 recipe Chunky Bleu Cheese Dressing (*recipe follows*)
1 recipe Toasted Spiced Walnuts (*recipe follows*)
1 pound cooked applewood smoked bacon, crumbled

CHUNKY BLEU CHEESE DRESSING
Makes about 3 cups
1 cup mayonnaise
½ cup sour cream
6 tablespoons buttermilk
1½ tablespoons chopped garlic
1 tablespoon fresh lemon juice
1½ tablespoons Worcestershire sauce
8 ounces crumbled bleu cheese
Kosher salt, to taste

SPICED WALNUTS
Makes 2 cups
2 cups small walnut nuggets
2 tablespoons unsalted butter
3 tablespoons Worcestershire sauce
¼ teaspoon Tabasco sauce
1 teaspoon kosher salt

When doing research for Cotton's opening menu, I browsed through hundreds of old menus, some dating as far back as the '30s. A simple salad consisting of a wedge of iceberg lettuce with a creamy dressing appeared on lots of menus. I decided that I would "reinvent the wedge" as Cotton's signature salad. My dressing of choice would be chunky bleu cheese and garnishments of spiced walnuts and applewood smoked bacon. This salad has been on our menu ever since, unchanged from the first night it made its debut at Cotton 8 years ago.

Place 1 wedge of iceberg lettuce on each serving plate. Top with bleu cheese dressing and sprinkle with toasted spiced walnuts and crumbled bacon. Serve immediately.

CHUNKY BLEU CHEESE DRESSING
In a large mixing bowl, combine the mayonnaise, sour cream, buttermilk, lemon juice, and Worcestershire sauce together, blending well. Fold in the crumbled bleu cheese. Season to taste with kosher salt. Cover and refrigerate, will keep up to 5 days.

SPICED WALNUTS
Preheat the oven to 300°F. Line a sheet pan with parchment paper. In a saucepan, heat the butter, Worcestershire sauce, and Tabasco sauce over medium heat. When the butter has melted, stir in the nuts. Cook, stirring constantly, until all of the liquid has been absorbed by the nuts, 4 to 5 minutes. Transfer the nuts to the sheet pan and spread into an even single layer. Bake in the oven for 20 to 30 minutes, until the nuts are golden-brown. Remove from the oven and sprinkle with kosher salt. Allow the nuts to cool to room temperature and store in an airtight container at room temperature for up to 5 days.

Lemongrass Chicken Salad

over Asian Veggie Slaw

SERVES 6

Six 5- to 6-ounce boneless, skinless chicken breasts
1 recipe Chicken Marinade (*recipe follows*)
1 recipe Asian Veggie Slaw (*recipe follows*)
1 recipe Ginger Aioli (*recipe follows*)

CHICKEN MARINADE
1 tablespoon chopped garlic
1 tablespoon chopped lemongrass
2 tablespoons sugar
¼ cup fish sauce
¼ cup vegetable oil

ASIAN VEGGIE SLAW
½ head napa cabbage, outer leaves removed
½ cup bean sprouts
½ cup shredded carrots
½ cup thinly sliced sweet red bell pepper
½ cup thinly sliced snow peas
1 recipe Asian Vinaigrette (*recipe follows*)
Kosher salt and fresh-ground black pepper, to taste

ASIAN VINAIGRETTE
Makes about 1 cup
1½ tablespoons minced gingerroot
3 tablespoons sugar
¼ cup sesame oil
¼ cup rice wine vinegar
¼ cup soy sauce

GINGER AIOLI
1½ tablespoons chopped gingerroot
3 scallions, thinly sliced, greens only
1½ teaspoons sugar
1½ teaspoons sesame oil
1½ teaspoons soy sauce
1½ cups mayonnaise

The city of Manchester holds a "Taste of Downtown" festival every September, in which downtown restaurants are paired with downtown merchants. The first year Cotton participated, I made this salad as one of our sample dishes. It was a big hit, and we received several requests to put it on our regular lunch menu.

Gently pound the chicken breasts between wax paper or plastic wrap to even thickness. In a large mixing bowl, toss the chicken with the marinade, cover and refrigerate 2 to 3 hours. Preheat your outdoor grill. Grill the chicken breasts until done. To serve, evenly divide the Asian slaw among the serving plates. Top each with a hot chicken breast or grilled and chilled slices of chicken. Drizzle aioli over each salad, or serve on the side.

CHICKEN MARINADE
Combine all of the ingredients in a mixing bowl and blend well. Cover and refrigerate up to 3 days.

ASIAN VEGGIE SLAW
In a large mixing bowl, combine all of the vegetables and toss well. Cover and refrigerate. The vegetables can be prepared to this point up to 4 hours before serving. Toss the vegetables with the Asian Vinaigrette, and season to taste with kosher salt and black pepper.

ASIAN VINAIGRETTE
Combine all of the ingredients in a mixing bowl and blend well. Cover and refrigerate up to 3 days. Stir well before serving.

GINGER AIOLI
In the work bowl of a food processor, combine the gingerroot, scallions, and sugar. Process until finely chopped. Add the remaining ingredients and pulse until ingredients are combined well. Cover and refrigerate until needed, up to 2 days.

═ Entrées ═

Comfort food, as its name suggests, reduces stress and takes us back to that happy place called home. Whether it's a simple grilled steak for a birthday dinner, Mom's meatloaf with mashed potatoes, or buttermilk fried chicken, such dishes are tied to times, places, and special memories for most of us. Many of the main course dishes at Cotton are considered fine dining comfort foods. Using all-natural meats, wild-caught fish and shellfish, and local, certified-organic produce, we recreate old-fashioned favorites, meals that provide familiarity and emotional security. Dishes like our Almond-Crusted Turkey Schnitzel, Southern-Style Buttermilk Fried Chicken, Meatloaf with Buttery Mashed Potatoes, and Grilled Brandt All-Natural Ribeye Beefsteak have been mainstays on Cotton's menu for the past eight years.

Almond Crusted Turkey Schnitzel

with Vermont Cheddar and Bourbon Applesauce   SERVES 4

TURKEY SCHNITZEL
2½ cups fresh breadcrumbs
½ cup slivered blanched almonds, roughly chopped
½ teaspoon kosher salt
½ teaspoon fresh-ground black pepper
⅓ cup all-purpose flour
3 large eggs, beaten for egg wash
Four 4- to 5-ounce turkey cutlets, gently pounded to
    an even thickness
⅓ cup vegetable oil
Four ¾-ounce slices of Vermont cheddar cheese
1 recipe Chunky Bourbon Applesauce (recipe follows)
2 tablespoons toasted slivered almonds for garnish

CHUNKY BOURBON APPLESAUCE
2½ pounds Granny Smith apples, peeled and cored
3 tablespoons light brown sugar
¾ cup bourbon

In January 2004, I was asked to join the National Turkey Federation in launching a new initiative, "Turkey, Savor the Success," a web feature series on www.eatturkey.com, highlighting the expanding popularity of turkey throughout the food service marketplace.

This recipe is the dish I created for that occasion. Over 4 years later, this dish is still a recurring feature recipe on www.eatturkey.com, and a signature dish on Cotton's dinner menu.

Mix the fresh breadcrumbs, chopped almonds, salt, and pepper in a shallow container. Place flour and beaten eggs (egg wash) into two additional individual shallow containers. Dredge each turkey cutlet in the flour, egg wash, and finally the almond-breadcrumb mixture.

Preheat the oven to 400°F. Heat the oil in a large sauté pan over medium heat. Brown the breaded cutlets, being careful not to crowd the pan. Cook until golden-brown, approximately 3 to 4 minutes on each side. Transfer the cutlets to a sheet pan. Top each cutlet with a slice of cheddar cheese and 2 tablespoons of applesauce. Bake 5 to 6 minutes. Sprinkle with toasted almonds and serve immediately.

CHUNKY BOURBON APPLESAUCE
Dice apples into ½-inch dice. In a heavy saucepan, combine the apples, brown sugar, and bourbon. Cook over medium-low heat, stirring often, for about 20 to 30 minutes, or until the apples are soft. Stir vigorously to mash the apples. The applesauce may be served warm or cooled completely and refrigerated, tightly covered, up to 5 days.

Southern-Style Buttermilk Fried Chicken

with Herbed Cream Gravy

SERVES 6 TO 8

Eight 4- to 5-ounce boneless, skinless chicken breasts
3 cups buttermilk
2 cups all-purpose flour
1 tablespoon kosher salt
1 teaspoon fresh-ground black pepper
2 teaspoons onion powder
1 teaspoon garlic powder
2 teaspoons dried thyme
2 teaspoons dried rubbed sage
1 teaspoon dried sweet basil

Vegetable oil for frying
1 recipe Herbed Cream Gravy (recipe follows)

HERBED CREAM GRAVY
Makes about 3 cups
3 tablespoons unsalted butter
1 tablespoon minced shallots
½ teaspoon minced garlic
3 tablespoons all-purpose flour
2 cups chicken stock
1 teaspoon chopped fresh parsley
1 teaspoon chopped fresh thyme
1 teaspoon chopped fresh tarragon
1 cup heavy cream
Kosher salt and ground white pepper, to taste

This recipe goes back to the days when I was the chef of The Creamery at Canterbury Shaker Village. Inspired by the Shaker's of Pleasant Hill, Kentucky, this dish is pure American comfort food at its best. Soaking the chicken in buttermilk overnight intensifies the flavor and ensures tender, juicy chicken.

Gently pound the chicken breasts between wax paper or plastic wrap to even thickness. In a large bowl, soak the chicken in the buttermilk overnight, covered in the refrigerator. Preheat the oven to 225°F, and line a sheet pan with paper towels. Heat an electric fryer to 350°F, or in a large Dutch oven, heat 3 inches of vegetable oil to 350°F (use a deep fat frying thermometer) over medium-high heat. In another large bowl, thoroughly combine the flour, salt, pepper, onion powder, garlic powder, and herbs. Remove each piece of chicken from the buttermilk, shaking off excess, and dredge in the seasoned flour. Shake off the excess flour. Carefully lower the chicken into the hot oil, careful not to overcrowd the pot. Cook the chicken until golden-brown, 5 to 6 minutes. Turn the chicken during cooking for even browning, if necessary. When the chicken is cooked, carefully remove it to the paper towel-lined sheet pan. Hold in the 225° oven while you cook the remaining chicken. When all of the chicken is cooked, serve immediately with the gravy.

HERBED CREAM GRAVY
In a large heavy saucepan, melt the butter over medium-low heat. Add the shallots and garlic, and cook 2 to 3 minutes without allowing them to color. Add the flour and stir to form a paste. Cook for 3 to 4 minutes, stirring, being careful not to allow the paste to brown. Stir in the stock until smooth. Stir over medium heat until the sauce thickens; simmer for 10 to 15 minutes, stirring often. Stir in the herbs and cream, and season with kosher salt and ground white pepper to taste. Serve hot.

Meatloaf

with Wild Mushroom Port Wine Sauce   Serves 6 to 8

MEATLOAF

1 tablespoon chopped garlic

2 tablespoons onion powder

¼ cup Worcestershire sauce

1 tablespoon kosher salt

4 extra large eggs

2½ pounds ground beef, preferably 80/20

2½ pounds ground pork

1½ cups old fashioned rolled oats

WILD MUSHROOM PORT WINE SAUCE

1 tablespoon vegetable oil

8 ounces white mushrooms, sliced

4 ounces shiitake mushrooms, stems removed, then sliced

8 ounces portobello mushrooms, stems and gills removed,
    then sliced

2 cups port wine

4 cups demi-glace or beef gravy[1]

Kosher salt and fresh-ground black pepper, to taste

There's something about meatloaf and mashed potatoes that makes me feel welcome and at home when I see them on the dinner table. This dish has been on Cotton's menu since day one. We serve it with All You Can Eat Mashed Potatoes. The mashed potatoes (*see page 59*) are a very important part of this meal, perfect for soaking up the accompanying sauce.

Preheat the oven to 375°F. In a blender, combine the garlic, onion powder, Worcestershire sauce, salt, and eggs, and blend well. In a large mixing bowl, combine the ground beef, ground pork, oats, and the liquids. Mix by hand gently, just until all the ingredients are incorporated. Divide the mixture in half, shape into two loafs and place in a large baking pan. Bake in the preheated oven for 50 to 60 minutes. Remove from the oven and allow the meatloaf to rest for 10 to 15 minutes before serving.

WILD MUSHROOM PORT WINE SAUCE

In a large saucepan, heat the vegetable oil over high heat. When the oil begins to smoke, carefully add all the mushrooms. Cook until the mushrooms start to wilt. Add the port wine, simmering the mushrooms until almost all of the liquid has evaporated, about 15 to 20 minutes. Add the demi-glace, heat to a boil, then simmer for 5 minutes, stirring often. Season with kosher salt and black pepper to taste. Pour over sliced meatloaf and serve.

[1] *Demi-glace can be found in the specialty section of many grocery stores or purchased online at www.bonewerksculinarte.com.*

Grilled Brandt All-Natural Ribeye Beefsteak

with Smoky Bacon Bleu Cheese Butter

<u>SMOKY BACON BLEU CHEESE BUTTER</u>
1 pound unsalted butter, room temperature
½ pound cooked bacon, crumbled
1 tablespoon chopped garlic
One 4-ounce container crumbled bleu cheese
3 scallions, thinly sliced, greens only
Kosher salt and fresh-ground black pepper, to taste

About 5 years ago, I made the decision to serve only all-natural beef. After several tastings, and background checks on the ranchers, I decided on Brandt Beef ~ The True Natural. Brandt Family Farm is located in Brawley, California. They raise their cattle naturally, the way Mother Nature intended. Unlike conventional cattle growers, Brandt Beef doesn't use growth hormones or antibiotics in their feed diet. This natural feeding process, and the best and most humane techniques of animal husbandry known today, produce the most consistently tender and flavorful beef in the country. The steaks we serve at Cotton are unparalleled in taste, tenderness, and consistency.

Visit Brandt Beef online at www.brandtbeef.com, your local meat shop, or farmer's market and pick up your favorite grilling cut of all-natural beef. This flavored butter also goes well with grilled chicken, pork chops, and veal chops.

<u>SMOKEY BACON BLEU CHEESE BUTTER</u>
In the bowl of a mixer, whip the butter until smooth. Add the remaining ingredients, mixing just until the ingredients are combined well. Season to taste with kosher salt and fresh-ground black pepper. Using a piece of wax paper, parchment paper, or plastic food film, spread the butter into a long strip. Roll the butter back and forth to form an even cylinder. Twist the ends to seal. Refrigerate until service. The butter may also be frozen up to 1 month. To serve, slice into ¼-inch thick rounds and place on top of hot grilled steak, chicken, or pork chops.

Grilled Jumbo Scallops

with Applewood Smoked Bacon, Spring Peas, Pea Tendrils, and Green Garlic Herb Oil

3 pounds U-10 jumbo dry pack sea scallops
  (*8 ounces per person*)
1 pound applewood smoked bacon, cooked and crumbled
1 small sweet onion, peeled, cut in half, and thinly sliced
1 cup fresh or frozen sweet peas
¼ pound fresh pea tendrils (available at farmer's markets
  and Asian markets)
3 tablespoons vegetable oil
1 recipe Mashed Potatoes (*recipe follows*)
1 recipe Green Garlic Herb Oil (*recipe follows*)
Kosher salt and fresh-ground black pepper, to taste

MASHED POTATOES

2 pounds Maine, Yukon gold, or red potatoes, washed
1 stick unsalted butter, cut into small pieces
1 tablespoon chopped garlic
1 cup warm milk or heavy cream
Kosher salt and ground white pepper, to taste

GREEN GARLIC HERB OIL

Makes about 1¼ cups
⅓ cup curly parsley sprigs, stems removed, loosely packed
⅓ cup cilantro leaves, loosely packed
⅓ cup Genovese basil leaves, loosely packed
1 teaspoon chopped garlic
1 level teaspoon ground cumin
1 level teaspoon ground coriander
½ teaspoon kosher salt
½ cup vegetable oil
¼ cup white wine vinegar

Preheat your outdoor grill. Toss the scallops in a bowl with 2 tablespoons vegetable oil and season with kosher salt and black pepper. Grill the scallops to desired doneness, serve immediately.

In a large sauté pan or wok, heat 1 tablespoon of vegetable oil over high heat. Add the sliced onions, peas, and pea tendrils and cook very quickly (stir-fry). Add the crumbled bacon and season to taste with kosher salt and black pepper. Serve immediately.

To serve, place mashed potatoes in the center of each dinner plate, top the mashed potatoes with the stir-fried vegetable-bacon mixture. Arrange the grilled scallops around the potatoes and drizzle with the Green Garlic Herb Oil.

MASHED POTATOES

Bring a large pot of lightly salted water to a boil over high heat. Peel and quarter the potatoes, and cook in the boiling water until tender, about 30 minutes. Drain well. Return the potatoes to the pot and cook over low heat to dry out any remaining moisture in the potatoes. Begin to mash the potatoes, mixing in the garlic, butter, and milk, being careful not to overmix the potatoes. Season to taste with kosher salt and ground white pepper. Serve immediately.

GREEN GARLIC HERB OIL

Combine all ingredients in a blender and process until smooth. Refrigerate until needed. Stir well, to emulsify, before serving.

= Martinis =

In the pre-opening planning of Cotton, we decided early on to apply just as much focus and attention to detail to our cocktail menu as we did to our food. Our goal was to offer classic cocktails, properly prepared, served in the proper glass, with the proper garnish. With the advent of ultra-premium and infused vodkas, Peaches, my wife and partner, decided to stray a little from the original martini recipe—gin and dry vermouth—and experiment with vodka-based "new" martinis. The rest, as they say, is history. She and Cotton have held the distinct honor of "Best Martinis in New Hampshire" from *New Hampshire Magazine* for the past five years. Here are the six simple steps to a perfect martini, along with recipes for five of Cotton's signature "new" martinis.

<u>STEPS TO A PERFECT MARTINI</u>

1st   Chill your martini glass by filling it with ice cubes and water and letting it sit while you make the martini

2nd   Fill a cocktail shaker with ice, then add all liquid ingredients and shake vigorously

3rd   Empty the ice and water from the martini glass

4th   Rim the glass with the appropriate rimmer—sugar, salt, etc.

5th   Strain the contents of the cocktail shaker into the chilled martini glass

6th   Garnish and serve

Pomegranate

2 ounces Pearl Pomegranate vodka
1 ounce triple sec
2 ounces Langer's 100 percent pomegranate cocktail juice
Stirrings Pomegranate sugared rimmer

There are a lot of pomegranate liqueurs that you can use, though I find that the addition of pomegranate juice makes the best martini. Feel free to use whatever pomegranate vodka you prefer.

Stirrings sugared rimmer garnishes can be found in the specialty section of many grocery stores or purchased online at www.stirrings.com.

Toasted Coconut

2 ounces Brinley's Vanilla Rum
1 ounce Frangelico
1 ounce Fabbri Italian Coconut Syrup
1 teaspoon toasted coconut (*garnish*)

If you can't find the Brinley's Vanilla Rum, you can make your own. Cut a vanilla bean in half lengthwise, scrape out the seeds, and add them along with the pod to a bottle of dark rum. Allow the rum to age a minimum of 24 hours before serving.

Coconut syrup can be purchased online at www.fabbri1905.com or www.monin.com or you may substitute with Coco Lopez.

Plum Sake

2 ounces Pearl Plum vodka
1 ounce sweet sake (Japanese rice wine)
½ ounce Monin Blackcurrant Syrup

Monin Blackcurrant Syrup may be purchased
online at www.monin.com or you may
substitute with crème de cassis liquer.

Lychee Tea

½ ounce vodka
½ ounce rum
½ ounce gin
½ ounce tequila
1 ounce triple sec
1 ounce pineapple juice
1 ounce Monin Lychee Syrup

Monin Lychee Syrup may be purchased online at www.monin.com or you may substitute with the syrup from a can of lychee nuts. Lychee nuts can be found at most Asian markets.

Fresh pineapple also makes a nice garnish for this martini.

Cherry Margarcia

2 ounces Patrón Silver tequila
1 ounce triple sec
1 ounce sour mix
Splash of maraschino cherry juice from a jar of cherries

You can certainly use whichever tequila you prefer, and can also substitute Cointreau for triple sec. Fresh cherries make a nice garnish.

= Acknowledgments =

Thanks to all our loyal guests who've joined us at the dinner table these past eight years. Without you, Cotton wouldn't be here.

Thanks to Cotton's wonderful staff, past and present: Scooter, Dwayne, Todd, Tim, Dan, Kim, Kerri, Tina, Lynn, George, James, Erika, Csilla, Steve, Matt, Antonia, Connie, Zurma, Jiva, Sydney, Karyn, Jessica, Dave, Michael, Meredith, Sara, and Jen. Your hard work every day makes Cotton one of New Hampshire's best restaurants.

Thanks to Brian Johnson, our former partner, for not giving up on our partnership and Cotton when the going got tough.

Thanks to James Haller, Jasper White, James Dodge, Julia Child, and Jacques Despres, my culinary mentors and treasured friends.

Thanks to New Hampshire's farmers, especially Eero Ruuttila, at Nesenkeag Farm, who was kind enough to take me on as his first restaurant account almost twenty years ago.

Thanks to Sun Chung, Michael Buckley, Tom Boucher, and Scott Ouellette, New Hampshire's finest independent restaurateurs, who are always there for me when I need them.

Thanks to John Clayton for uncovering the secret culinary history of Manchester's millyard in his colorful foreword.

Thanks to Brian Smestad, who has captured the essence of Cotton throughout these pages. You are truly gifted!

Thanks to Betty and Ken Paige, my mom and dad, who unconditionally never stop believing in Cotton and in me.

Finally, and most importantly, thanks to Peaches, my wife, love, and business partner. I couldn't do it without you.